God Wants Us to Listen

KATHRYN LUTZ

Edited by
Patricia H. Lemon

**Illustrated By
Justin Wager**

Graded Press

NASHVILLE

Copyright © 1986 by Kathryn Lutz
Art copyright © 1986 by Graded Press
All rights reserved.
ISBN 0-939697-03-3
Manufactured in the United States of America

DING DONG! The doorbell rings.
A friend has come; a ball he brings.
"Let's eat breakfast here today;
And then we'll go outside and play."

Ding dong . . .

So many sounds that I can hear!
Thank you, God, for my ears.

"WAAAH! WAAAH!" his sister cries.
He gives the ball to her and tries
To let her know that it's okay
For her to play with them all day.

Ding dong, Waaah waaah . . .

So many sounds that I can hear!
Thank you, God, for my ears.

CRACKLE, CRACKLE is the sound
Of bacon frying crisp and brown.
Let's start to eat; it's on the plate.
We're so hungry; let's not wait!

Ding dong, Waaah waaah, Crackle crackle . . .

So many sounds that I can hear!
Thank you, God, for my ears.

"YUM, YUMMMMM," is what we say.
What a good way to start our day!
Let's drink our juice and eat some more
Before we go to play outdoors.

Ding dong, Waaah waaah, Crackle crackle
Yum yummmmm . . .

So many sounds that I can hear!
Thank you, God, for my ears.

"TWEET, TWEET," sing the birds
With the sweetest sounds I have heard.
They fly so high, then come to rest
On top of our white garden fence.

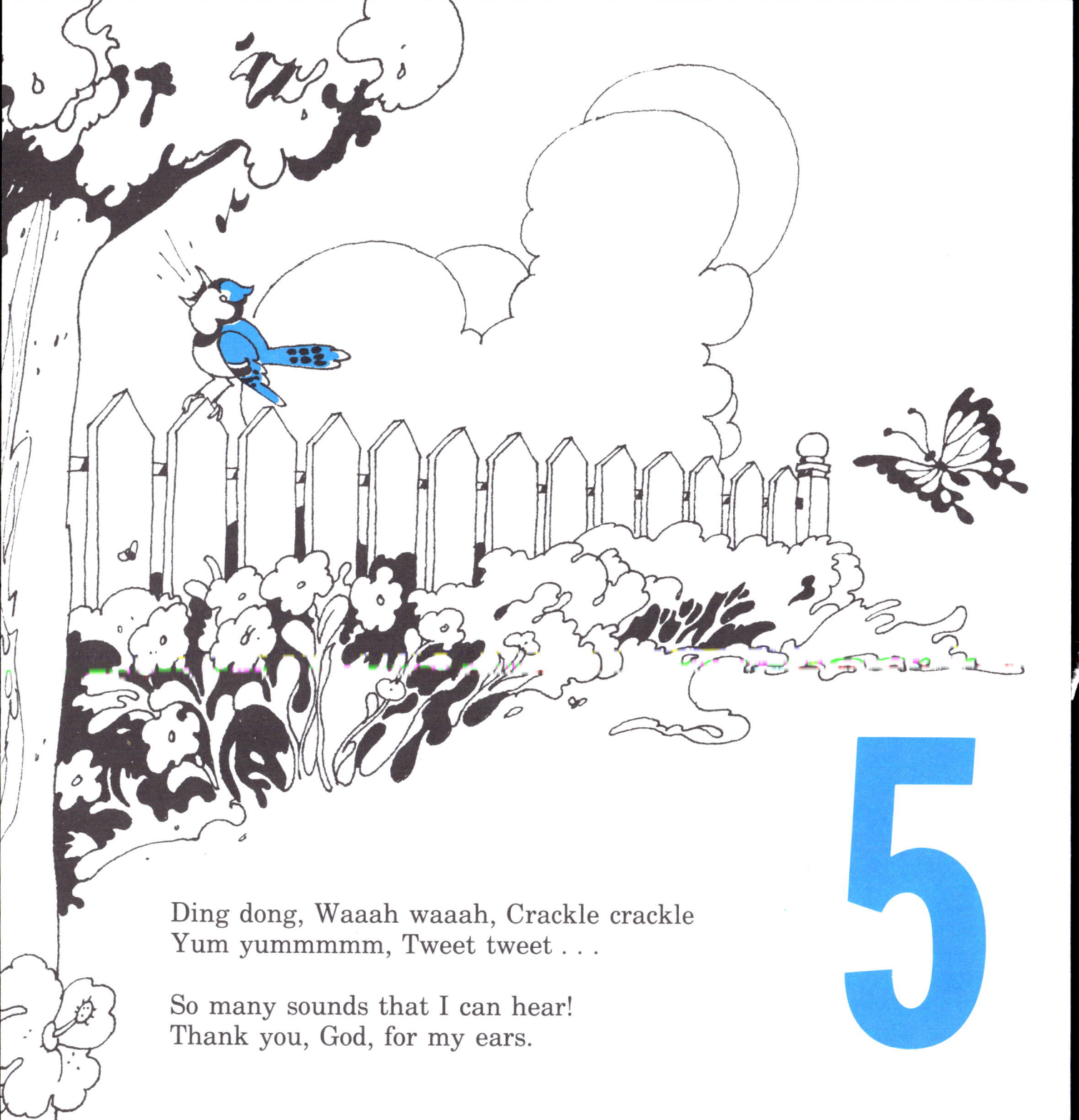

Ding dong, Waaah waaah, Crackle crackle
Yum yummmmm, Tweet tweet . . .

So many sounds that I can hear!
Thank you, God, for my ears.

5

"BUZZ, BUZZ," says a bee
As he flies so busily.
He looks for nectar, his daily food,
And finds it in the flowers that bloom.

Ding dong, Waaah waaah, Crackle crackle
Yum yummmmm, Tweet tweet, Buzz buzz . . .

So many sounds that I can hear!
Thank you, God, for my ears.

"PITTER PAT," sings the rain
As it falls on the window pane.
It's God's drink for living things;
It makes the garden grow in spring.

Ding dong, Waaah waaah, Crackle crackle
Yum yummmmm, Tweet tweet, Buzz buzz
Pitter pat . . .

So many sounds that I can hear!
Thank you, God, for my ears.

"QUACK, QUACK!" Mommy duck does say.
She calls her babies, "Come this way!
Get out of the rain and come in here.
We'll stay inside till the sky is clear."

Ding dong, Waaah waaah, Crackle crackle
Yum yummmmm, Tweet tweet, Buzz buzz
Pitter pat, Quack quack . . .

So many sounds that I can hear!
Thank you, God, for my ears.

8

"RUFF! RUFF!" the dog did cry.
"You're in my house that keeps me dry!
Please get out and go away.
Please find another place to stay!"

Ding dong, Waaah waaah, Crackle crackle
Yum yummmmm, Tweet tweet, Buzz buzz
Pitter pat, Quack quack, Ruff ruff . . .

So many sounds that I can hear!
Thank you, God, for my ears.

"SHHHHHHHH! SHHHHHHHH!"
Please be quiet! Please be still!
Please just listen, if you will,
To the sounds that I can hear.
Thank you, God, for my ears.

Ding dong, Waaah waaah, Crackle crackle
Yum yummmmm, Tweet tweet, Buzz buzz
Pitter pat, Quack quack, Ruff ruff
Shhhhhhhh shhhhhhh . . .

Make a joyful noise to the LORD,
   all the earth;
  break forth into joyous song and
   sing praises!

(Psalm 98:4)

To Parents and Teachers

God Wants Us to Listen is designed to help children grow in their appreciation for God's gifts of hearing and sound. They will be introduced to a Scripture verse that can be used in daily prayer and worship.

As you and your child enjoy reading *God Wants Us to Listen,* identify and review colors and numbers, name and count the colored objects, and name other parts of each picture. Identify the Scripture verse as coming from the Bible. Older children may enjoy seeing where the verse is found in the Bible. Repeat together the words of the Scripture verse. A prayer of thanksgiving may be appropriate.

Use of the audio cassette will enable children to repeat the story on their own.

Other titles in this series: *God Made the World We See, The Smells in God's World, God's Gift of Touch.*